ALA Survey of Librarian Salaries 1993

Mary Jo Lynch, *Project Director*
Margaret Myers
Jeniece Guy

ALA Survey Report

American Library Association
Office for Research and Statistics
Office for Library Personnel Resources

American Library Association
Chicago and London 1993

ISBN: 0-8389-7685-9
ISSN: 0747-7201

Acknowledgments

The authors wish to thank the many respondents who completed our questionnaires. Without their cooperation, this report would not be possible. We are grateful to the Association of Research Libraries (ARL) for sharing data with us as described in Appendix D and especially to Gordon Fretwell of the University of Massachusetts at Amherst who produced a printout of ARL data for us. We are also grateful to Chris Horak, Sara Suelflow, Sylvia Temperley, and other staff at the Library Research Center of the Graduate School of Library and Information Science at the University of Illinois who managed the mailings and processed the returns. Finally, thanks are due to Maxine Moore and Patricia A. Jackson for word processing the revised text and tables.

Table of Contents

Introduction

Librarians, the people who hire them, and interested others often ask the American Library Association (ALA) Office for Library Personnel Resources (OLPR) to tell them what salary might be paid to a librarian in a particular position, working in a particular type of library, in a particular part of the U.S. To fill the need for information of this kind, ALA began conducting a periodic survey of salaries for full-time professionals in academic and public libraries. Reports were published biennially from 1982 to 1988 and became annual in 1989.

This report, the ninth in a series, presents salaries paid to incumbents in six positions commonly found in U.S. academic and public libraries. Salaries were reported as of April 1, 1993. For each of five positions, the report contains six tables, one for each of five library types and one for all five combined. The sixth position--children's and/or young adult services librarian--is shown only for public libraries. Each of the tables shows the range, mean, first quartile, median, and third quartile of salaries in four geographic regions. Salaries paid to beginning professionals are also displayed in the same way.

The 1993 report shares the following characteristics with its immediate predecessor:

- It is based on a survey of **libraries**, not individual librarians.

- It is based on a survey of **full-time** positions.

- It is based on a survey of **public and academic** libraries only. (Sources for salaries in other libraries are given in Appendix A.)

- The public and academic library universe is stratified by the same **type/size criteria**: public libraries serving populations of from 25,000 to 99,999, public libraries serving populations of 100,000 or more, two-year colleges, four-year colleges, and universities. (The last category includes all institutions offering work beyond the bachelor's level).

- The nation is stratified into the same **geographic areas**: North Atlantic, Great Lakes and Plains, Southeast, West and Southwest (see Appendix D for list of states).

- It shows the **first quartile, median, and third quartile** for salaries paid in each type/size of library and region in addition to the mean and range (low and high) for each position reported.

- It shows salaries paid to staff **with master's degrees from graduate library education programs accredited by ALA.**

The last characteristic was added in the 1991 report. In previous years, the instructions asked for "professional" positions and quoted the definition of professional given in ALA's policy on "Library Education and Personnel Utilization." The wording was changed in 1991 because survey users indicated that data would be more useful if the degree was specified.

The 1993 survey differed from its predecessor in two minor ways. Previously, respondents were asked to report salaries paid as of January 1 of the survey year. Because of changes in the schedule for producing and publishing this report, respondents were asked to report salaries paid as of April 1, 1993. The April date will be used in subsequent surveys.

The second change is in the number of positions included. Previously, this survey requested salaries paid to "Collections Development Librarian/Subject Bibliographer." That position was dropped this year for two reasons. The number of incumbents was very small for two of the five library types (two-year college, four-year college) and small also for medium-sized public library. In recent years, respondents in libraries of all types and sizes have told us that duties in this position description were completed by people who also served in other positions, primarily Reference/Information Librarian. To better reflect this reality, small changes were made in the following position descriptions: Deputy/Associate/Assistant Director; Reference/Information Librarian; Children's and/or Young Adult Librarian.

The 1993 survey also contained four questions asked on a one-time-only basis:

1a. Did your library lay off paid staff because of budget cuts in the last 12 months?

      _____ yes_____ no

    1b. If yes, please provide number of full-time equivalent (FTE) staff laid off in the following categories:

        _____ staff with master's degrees from programs accredited by ALA

        _____ all other staff

2a. Did your library lose or freeze vacant positions in the last 12 months?

      _____ yes_____ no

    2b. If yes, please provide the number of full-time equivalent (FTE) positions in the following categories:

        _____ positions usually filled with staff holding master's degrees from programs accredited by ALA

        _____ positions usually filled with other staff

Twenty-seven academic libraries and thirty-four public libraries reported laying off staff because of budget cuts. Ninety-eight academic libraries and 124 public libraries reported that positions were lost or frozen. Additional details will appear in a forthcoming issue of *Library Personnel News*.

The Library Research Center of the University of Illinois Graduate School of Library and Information Science performed the mailing, processing, and computer analysis of the questionnaires. Mary Jo Lynch, Director of ALA's Office for Research and Statistics (ORS), directed the project and wrote this report with assistance from Margaret Myers, Director of ALA's Office for Library Personnel Resources (OLPR) and Jeniece Guy, OLPR Assistant Director. Myers was responsible for Appendix A, B, and C.

We hope the results of the survey will be useful to employers of librarians who need this information in administering an equitable pay plan and to librarians seeking employment or career advancement.

Results

The survey questionnaire was mailed to 1,243 randomly selected libraries on March 31, 1993. Samples were drawn from twenty groups of libraries formed by stratifying five type-of-library categories by four regions of the U. S. Appendix D describes how groups were formed and sampled. By the second week in June, useable responses had been received from 946 libraries, 76 percent of those sampled.

The results of this survey are presented on the following pages in seven sets of tables. The first five sets present salaries paid to incumbents in positions common to both public and academic libraries. Respondents were asked to report all full-time incumbents *with master's degrees from graduate library education programs accredited by ALA* except for beginning professionals, whose salaries are shown in a special table. There are three pages of tables for each position. The first table presents salaries paid in medium-sized public libraries, i.e., those serving between 25,000 and 99,999. For each of four regions of the country and for the nation as a whole, the table shows the number of positions reported (N), the lowest salary and the highest salary (range), the mean (arithmetic average), the first quartile, median, and third quartile. This pattern is repeated for large public libraries (i.e., those serving populations of 100,000 or more), and for libraries in two-year colleges, four-year colleges, and in universities (i.e., institutions offering work beyond the baccalaureate degree).

Following these five sets of tables is a smaller set for children's and/or young adult services librarian. For this position, tables are given only for the two sizes of public libraries and for all public libraries.

The last set of tables describes salaries paid to beginning professionals following the pattern set in the first six sets of tables.

The following example illustrates how to interpret the tables. In the first table for the position of director--the table presenting salaries paid in medium-sized public libraries--there were 83 salaries reported from the North Atlantic region. The lowest of these was $24,500 and the highest was $86,000. When all the salaries were added together and the result was divided by the total number (83) the average or mean was $50,788. When all the salaries were arrayed from low to high, 25 percent of them fell below $42,692, the first quartile, 50 percent fell below $48,700, the median, and 50 percent were above $48,700. Seventy-five percent fell below $57,200, the third quartile, and 25 percent were above that amount. The middle 50 percent of the salaries fell between $42,692 and $57,200.

Two caveats should be observed in reading the tables. The higher the number of cases (N), the more reliable the results of the sample in giving a true picture of the total population. When the number of cases is less than twenty-five, the results should be used with caution. This caution is especially applicable to the regional data for libraries where the number of professional staff is often small-- medium sized public libraries, four-year colleges, and two-year colleges. Another caveat is that when the mean and the median are not close together, the mean is being influenced by some unusual values. When the mean is much higher than the median, there are several very high salaries. When the mean is much lower than the median, there are several very low salaries.

Director

(Page 1 of 3)

Chief administrative officer of the library or library system. Plans and directs all aspects of the operation. May have job title such as Librarian or Head Librarian.

Medium-sized Public Library
(Serving a population of from 25,000 to 99,999)

	MEAN	FIRST QUARTILE	MEDIAN	THIRD QUARTILE
North Atlantic N=83 Range= $24,500-$86,000	50,788	42,692	48,700	57,200
Great Lakes & Plains N=77 Range= $24,860-$81,006	48,897	41,675	48,816	56,396
Southeast N=54 Range= $23,500-$60,968	37,979	32,755	36,250	42,000
West & Southwest N=44 Range= $29,290-$85,452	52,456	41,276	50,084	60,696
All Regions N=258 Range= $23,500-$86,000	47,827	37,961	46,000	54,991

Large Public Library
(Serving a population of 100,000 or more)

	MEAN	FIRST QUARTILE	MEDIAN	THIRD QUARTILE
North Atlantic N=34 Range= $35,000-$125,000	66,569	49,150	64,482	84,558
Great Lakes & Plains N=37 Range= $36,753-$102,375	67,133	51,500	64,380	84,100
Southeast N=48 Range= $27,000-$110,100	59,230	47,547	57,497	67,701
West & Southwest N=55 Range= $34,596-$103,910	67,904	52,993	70,524	79,068
All Regions N=174 Range= $27,000-$125,000	65,086	50,128	64,378	78,228

Chief administrative officer of the library or library system. Plans and directs all aspects of the operation. May have job title such as Librarian or Head Librarian.

Two-Year College

	MEAN	FIRST QUARTILE	MEDIAN	THIRD QUARTILE
North Atlantic N=32 Range=$24,000-$63,000	47,672	42,833	48,127	54,578
Great Lakes & Plains N=28 Range=$21,500-$82,133	49,104	39,000	47,843	57,236
Southeast N=40 Range= $25,000-$69,387	43,076	35,182	42,750	48,500
West & Southwest N=32 Range= $30,500-$69,333	46,760	38,863	47,861	52,477
All Regions N=132 Range= $21,500-$82,133	46,362	38,385	46,000	53,177

Four-Year College

	MEAN	FIRST QUARTILE	MEDIAN	THIRD QUARTILE
North Atlantic N=30 Range=$25,848-$71,685	43,591	36,000	43,150	48,992
Great Lakes & Plains N=30 Range=$27,500-$71,000	42,958	32,435	40,575	53,000
Southeast N=29 Range=$20,000-$57,500	35,641	27,000	34,000	39,008
West & Southwest N=24 Range=$23,000-$85,050	45,062	34,150	41,000	52,167
All Regions N=113 Range= $20,000-$85,050	41,695	32,435	38,950	50,000

Chief administrative officer of the library or library system. Plans and directs all aspects of the operation. May have job title such as Librarian or Head Librarian.

University

	MEAN	FIRST QUARTILE	MEDIAN	THIRD QUARTILE
North Atlantic N=58 Range=$28,139-$160,000	65,260	49,400	64,801	75,000
Great Lakes & Plains N=65 Range=$21,760-$119,100	58,722	40,500	59,089	69,823
Southeast N=52 Range=$21,000-$92,941	55,758	41,231	58,500	66,561
West & Southwest N=53 Range=$28,500-$115,000	61,657	43,500	61,338	79,000
All Regions N=228 Range=$21,000-$160,000	60,391	42,938	60,000	73,108

All Academic and Public Libraries

	MEAN	FIRST QUARTILE	MEDIAN	THIRD QUARTILE
North Atlantic N=237 Range=$24,000-$160,000	55,262	43,000	51,592	64,375
Great Lakes & Plains N=237 Range=$21,500-$119,100	53,711	40,108	51,414	63,137
Southeast N=223 Range=$20,000-$110,100	47,309	35,000	42,700	57,500
West & Southwest N=208 Range=$23,000-$115,000	57,156	41,876	53,401	72,775
All Regions N=905 Range=$20,000-$160,000	53,331	39,962	50,000	63,221

SOURCE: ALA SURVEY OF LIBRARIAN SALARIES, 1993

Deputy/Associate/Assistant Director

Aids Director in planning and directing some or all aspects of library or library system. May manage a major aspect of the library operation (e.g., technical services, public services, collection development, systems/automation).

Medium-sized Public Library
(Serving a population of from 25,000 to 99,999)

	MEAN	FIRST QUARTILE	MEDIAN	THIRD QUARTILE
North Atlantic N=56 Range=$24,330-$68,782	41,174	34,610	40,250	45,820
Great Lakes & Plains N=48 Range=$20,591-$65,137	37,540	31,872	36,573	42,306
Southeast N=28 Range=$20,567-$52,268	31,667	26,283	29,123	35,403
West & Southwest N=24 Range=$23,735-$64,884	40,167	30,545	39,246	48,615
All Regions N=156 Range=$20,567-$68,782	38,194	30,267	37,130	44,098

Large Public Library
(Serving a population of 100,000 or more)

	MEAN	FIRST QUARTILE	MEDIAN	THIRD QUARTILE
North Atlantic N=60 Range=$27,563-$100,000	60,812	48,249	62,681	69,129
Great Lakes & Plains N=53 Range=$32,240-$79,704	54,083	43,752	54,320	63,998
Southeast N=88 Range=$24,831-$71,064	44,548	35,230	44,820	51,165
West & Southwest N=97 Range=$25,848-$87,061	54,235	43,483	54,672	66,108
All Regions N=298 Range=$24,831-$100,000	52,672	41,773	51,792	63,197

SOURCE: ALA SURVEY OF LIBRARIAN SALARIES, 1993

Aids Director in planning and directing some or all aspects of library or library system. May manage a major aspect of the library operation (e.g., technical services, public services, collection development, systems/automation).

Two-Year College

	MEAN	FIRST QUARTILE	MEDIAN	THIRD QUARTILE
North Atlantic N=9 Range=$22,000-$72,763	41,982	31,200	38,077	48,000
Great Lakes & Plains N=7 Range=$30,000-$64,790	40,651	31,200	36,722	46,608
Southeast N=7 Range=$30,000-$44,749	35,536	30,000	33,000	43,000
West & Southwest N=15 Range=$25,259-$60,000	40,793	28,627	38,287	50,963
All Regions N=38 Range=$22,000-$72,763	40,080	30,390	37,027	47,353

Four-Year College

	MEAN	FIRST QUARTILE	MEDIAN	THIRD QUARTILE
North Atlantic N=12 Range=$23,078-$54,900	31,128	26,465	28,568	32,944
Great Lakes & Plains N=6 Range=$24,000-$48,403	39,126	32,510	42,158	45,525
Southeast N=9 Range=$20,388-$35,500	27,955	24,000	28,600	32,400
West & Southwest N=15 Range=$21,500-$64,872	36,782	27,000	31,368	55,348
All Regions N=42 Range=$20,388-$64,872	33,610	26,500	30,150	35,500

SOURCE: ALA SURVEY OF LIBRARIAN SALARIES, 1993

Deputy/Associate/Assistant Director (Page 3 of 3)

Aids Director in planning and directing some or all aspects of library or library system. May manage a major aspect of the library operation (e.g., technical services, public services, collection development, systems/automation).

University

	MEAN	FIRST QUARTILE	MEDIAN	THIRD QUARTILE
North Atlantic N=87 Range=$29,145-$102,288	54,291	46,537	52,915	62,000
Great Lakes & Plains N=69 Range=$20,280-$70,189	48,260	40,365	48,467	59,306
Southeast N=61 Range=$25,000-$79,104	43,475	35,000	43,464	50,000
West & Southwest N=86 Range=$24,710-$76,900	47,712	38,783	47,972	55,957
All Regions N=303 Range=$20,280-$102,288	48,873	40,800	48,960	56,500

All Academic and Public Libraries

	MEAN	FIRST QUARTILE	MEDIAN	THIRD QUARTILE
North Atlantic N=224 Range=$22,000-$102,288	51,023	39,315	49,277	62,000
Great Lakes & Plains N=183 Range=$20,280-$79,704	46,544	35,914	44,574	56,175
Southeast N=193 Range=$20,388-$79,104	41,240	32,074	40,300	49,046
West & Southwest N=237 Range=$21,500-$87,061	48,488	37,378	48,000	57,600
All Regions N=837 Range=$20,280-$102,288	47,070	35,976	45,985	56,161

SOURCE: ALA SURVEY OF LIBRARIAN SALARIES, 1993

Department Head/Branch Head
(Page 1 of 3)

Manages operation of a library unit that is physically separate from the main library (e.g., a branch or a department library) or of one aspect of the main library (e.g., Reference Department, Serials Department, Children's Department).

Medium-sized Public Library
(Serving a population of from 25,000 to 99,999)

	MEAN	FIRST QUARTILE	MEDIAN	THIRD QUARTILE
North Atlantic N=122 Range=$18,515-$56,664	36,543	29,500	36,334	41,161
Great Lakes & Plains N=163 Range=$20,100-$72,304	34,178	29,000	32,920	38,600
Southeast N=51 Range=$18,385-$47,771	28,767	23,675	26,780	32,698
West & Southwest N=74 Range=$19,089-$58,872	37,431	29,931	37,595	44,088
All Regions N=410 Range=$18,385-$72,304	34,795	28,618	33,509	40,044

Large Public Library
(Serving a population of 100,000 or more)

	MEAN	FIRST QUARTILE	MEDIAN	THIRD QUARTILE
North Atlantic N=546 Range=$19,300-$69,506	42,536	37,544	43,281	46,733
Great Lakes & Plains N=474 Range=$22,048-$57,772	39,845	35,807	39,032	43,222
Southeast N=410 Range=$17,088-$64,909	35,748	29,323	36,053	41,600
West & Southwest N=467 Range=$20,340-$79,682	40,617	34,008	40,008	46,959
All Regions N=1,897 Range=$17,088-$79,682	39,924	34,128	39,809	45,132

SOURCE: ALA SURVEY OF LIBRARIAN SALARIES, 1993

Manages operation of a library unit that is physically separate from the main library (e.g., a branch or a department library) or of one aspect of the main library (e.g., Reference Department, Serials Department, Children's Department).

Two-Year College

	MEAN	FIRST QUARTILE	MEDIAN	THIRD QUARTILE
North Atlantic N=13 Range=$35,000-$67,559	48,371	40,000	43,672	58,645
Great Lakes & Plains N=4 Range=$36,000-$80,824	61,200	46,788	63,988	75,612
Southeast N=15 Range=$21,500-$51,066	34,085	28,800	34,000	38,000
West & Southwest N=4 Range=$23,100-$42,632	33,048	26,751	33,230	39,345
All Regions N=36 Range=$21,500-$80,824	42,141	33,500	38,012	47,833

Four-Year College

	MEAN	FIRST QUARTILE	MEDIAN	THIRD QUARTILE
North Atlantic N=23 Range=$30,285-$67,800	42,323	34,832	42,240	45,988
Great Lakes & Plains N=28 Range=$21,820-$57,295	37,745	32,988	36,997	43,675
Southeast N=16 Range=$25,425-$43,094	33,074	28,050	33,308	34,973
West & Southwest N=27 Range=$20,500-$57,762	36,254	29,559	34,650	39,544
All Regions N=94 Range=$20,500-$67,800	37,642	30,792	36,084	43,000

SOURCE: ALA SURVEY OF LIBRARIAN SALARIES, 1993

Department Head/Branch Head (Page 3 of 3)

Manages operation of a library unit that is physically separate from the main library (e.g., a branch or a department library) or of one aspect of the main library (e.g., Reference Department, Serials Department, Children's Department).

University

	MEAN	FIRST QUARTILE	MEDIAN	THIRD QUARTILE
North Atlantic N=275 Range=$18,839-$103,000	41,197	34,485	40,279	47,500
Great Lakes & Plains N=306 Range=$23,475-$73,130	41,768	35,235	40,880	47,220
Southeast N=175 Range=$18,900-$63,137	35,334	30,000	36,036	39,900
West & Southwest N=262 Range=$21,656-$70,272	40,492	34,920	38,887	45,311
All Regions N=1,018 Range=$18,839-$103,000	40,179	34,370	39,240	45,692

All Academic and Public Libraries

	MEAN	FIRST QUARTILE	MEDIAN	THIRD QUARTILE
North Atlantic N=979 Range=$18,515-$103,000	41,486	35,400	41,892	46,400
Great Lakes & Plains N=975 Range=$20,100-$80,824	39,529	33,560	38,480	44,268
Southeast N=667 Range=$17,088-$64,909	35,004	28,367	35,283	40,047
West & Southwest N=834 Range=$19,089-$79,682	40,117	33,924	39,128	46,510
All Regions N=3,455 Range=$17,088-$103,000	39,352	33,280	38,781	44,755

SOURCE: ALA SURVEY OF LIBRARIAN SALARIES, 1993

Reference/Information Librarian
(Page 1 of 3)

Locates information for library users or helps users find it in print materials, automated databases, or other sources. Answers questions and gives instruction about the use of the library. Selects materials for the reference collection and general collections.

Medium-sized Public Library
(Serving a population of from 25,000 to 99,999)

	MEAN	FIRST QUARTILE	MEDIAN	THIRD QUARTILE
North Atlantic N=141 Range=$19,102-$56,664	33,145	27,930	32,257	37,357
Great Lakes & Plains N=140 Range=$18,637-$70,406	30,459	25,476	28,863	32,280
Southeast N=34 Range=$20,000-$41,946	25,805	21,834	23,451	26,000
West & Southwest N=51 Range=$24,937-$45,620	33,609	26,722	32,772	40,500
All Regions N=366 Range=$18,637-$70,406	31,501	25,854	30,323	35,391

Large Public Library
(Serving a population of 100,000 or more)

	MEAN	FIRST QUARTILE	MEDIAN	THIRD QUARTILE
North Atlantic N=561 Range=$17,300-$54,790	33,731	29,145	33,920	36,738
Great Lakes & Plains N=511 Range=$19,593-$46,150	31,713	28,886	30,454	34,270
Southeast N=331 Range=$20,509-$44,988	29,959	25,459	29,688	33,492
West & Southwest N=549 Range=$19,898-$48,776	33,994	29,987	33,012	38,358
All Regions N=1,952 Range=$17,300-$54,790	32,637	28,800	32,218	36,538

SOURCE: ALA SURVEY OF LIBRARIAN SALARIES, 1993

Reference/Information Librarian (Page 2 of 3)

Locates information for library users or helps users find it in print materials, automated databases, or other sources. Answers questions and gives instruction about the use of the library. Selects materials for the reference collection and general collections.

Two-Year College

	MEAN	FIRST QUARTILE	MEDIAN	THIRD QUARTILE
North Atlantic N=48 Range=$21,500-$88,384	41,644	33,604	38,028	45,250
Great Lakes & Plains N=38 Range=$21,500-$85,349	50,637	36,740	50,112	62,993
Southeast N=31 Range=$20,406-$54,609	37,531	31,836	36,500	44,847
West & Southwest N=30 Range=$18,000-$65,333	41,022	29,285	42,953	49,344
All Regions N=147 Range=$18,000-$88,384	42,974	33,500	40,000	50,112

Four-Year College

	MEAN	FIRST QUARTILE	MEDIAN	THIRD QUARTILE
North Atlantic N=34 Range=$19,400-$53,409	31,501	27,900	31,333	36,000
Great Lakes & Plains N=32 Range=$20,637-$58,048	31,620	24,491	28,296	37,342
Southeast N=22 Range=$18,000-$34,000	25,857	22,000	25,100	30,000
West & Southwest N=28 Range=$20,000-$48,000	31,169	27,194	29,420	35,293
All Regions N=116 Range=$18,000-$58,048	30,383	24,684	28,944	34,518

SOURCE: ALA SURVEY OF LIBRARIAN SALARIES, 1993

Locates information for library users or helps users find it in print materials, automated databases, or other sources. Answers questions and gives instruction about the use of the library. Selects materials for the reference collection and general collections.

University

	MEAN	FIRST QUARTILE	MEDIAN	THIRD QUARTILE
North Atlantic N=231 Range=$15,493-$54,000	35,020	29,000	33,859	40,685
Great Lakes & Plains N=248 Range=$21,500-$70,636	33,707	27,896	32,020	37,668
Southeast N=211 Range=$20,157-$45,650	28,808	25,000	28,244	31,870
West & Southwest N=292 Range=$18,257-$70,272	34,168	26,676	31,464	38,852
All Regions N=982 Range=$15,493-$70,636	33,100	27,300	31,378	36,985

All Academic and Public Libraries

	MEAN	FIRST QUARTILE	MEDIAN	THIRD QUARTILE
North Atlantic N=1,015 Range=$15,493-$88,384	34,242	29,127	33,909	37,181
Great Lakes & Plains N=969 Range=$18,637-$85,349	32,781	28,074	30,764	35,483
Southeast N=629 Range=$18,000-$54,609	29,578	25,000	29,000	32,870
West & Southwest N=950 Range=$18,000-$70,272	34,166	28,494	32,845	38,973
All Regions N=3,563 Range=$15,493-$88,384	33,001	28,000	31,850	36,738

SOURCE: ALA SURVEY OF LIBRARIAN SALARIES, 1993

Cataloger and/or Classifier
(Page 1 of 3)

Organizes all types of material purchased by the library. Describes each item in standard format and assigns access points. Assigns subject headings and classification numbers. May use automated systems. May be involved with only descriptive cataloging or only subject cataloging/classification.

Medium-sized Public Library
(Serving a population of from 25,000 to 99,999)

	MEAN	FIRST QUARTILE	MEDIAN	THIRD QUARTILE
North Atlantic N=28 Range=$17,998-$56,664	33,433	27,788	32,230	38,086
Great Lakes & Plains N=25 Range=$17,826-$39,686	28,271	24,570	27,973	30,200
Southeast N=17 Range=$16,500-$37,973	25,855	21,000	23,909	27,930
West & Southwest N=21 Range=$18,500-$49,944	32,670	27,168	31,920	38,208
All Regions N=91 Range=$16,500-$56,664	30,423	24,570	28,912	36,298

Large Public Library
(Serving a population of 100,000 or more)

	MEAN	FIRST QUARTILE	MEDIAN	THIRD QUARTILE
North Atlantic N=63 Range=$20,500-$56,906	34,136	27,820	33,909	39,066
Great Lakes & Plains N=63 Range=$19,175-$54,444	31,487	27,885	31,325	34,070
Southeast N=53 Range=$20,223-$52,633	29,762	24,491	28,142	34,400
West & Southwest N=71 Range=$19,011-$48,713	33,548	28,944	32,544	38,148
All Regions N=250 Range=$19,011-$56,906	32,374	27,404	31,364	37,236

SOURCE: ALA SURVEY OF LIBRARIAN SALARIES, 1993

Organizes all types of material purchased by the library. Describes each item in standard format and assigns access points. Assigns subject headings and classification numbers. May use automated systems. May be involved with only descriptive cataloging or only subject cataloging/classification.

Two-Year College

	MEAN	FIRST QUARTILE	MEDIAN	THIRD QUARTILE
North Atlantic N=21 Range=$21,200-$64,200	39,881	31,320	35,000	50,888
Great Lakes & Plains N=13 Range=$32,880-$72,684	50,359	41,280	47,000	62,193
Southeast N=16 Range=$22,660-$52,815	34,406	26,624	34,850	39,528
West & Southwest N=13 Range=$26,521-$56,400	42,014	40,600	41,941	48,000
All Regions N=63 Range=$21,200-$72,684	41,093	31,527	38,466	48,944

Four-Year College

	MEAN	FIRST QUARTILE	MEDIAN	THIRD QUARTILE
North Atlantic N=20 Range=$21,577-$53,520	30,930	24,175	26,807	35,450
Great Lakes & Plains N=9 Range=$25,330-$40,908	32,795	27,800	33,915	37,653
Southeast N=14 Range=$20,000-$32,000	25,647	22,000	26,171	28,300
West & Southwest N=12 Range=$23,000-$53,316	33,778	25,491	32,612	39,518
All Regions N=55 Range=$20,000-$53,520	30,512	25,000	27,713	36,000

SOURCE: ALA SURVEY OF LIBRARIAN SALARIES, 1993

Cataloger and/or Classifier (Page 3 of 3)

Organizes all types of material purchased by the library. Describes each item in standard format and assigns access points. Assigns subject headings and classification numbers. May use automated systems. May be involved with only descriptive cataloging or only subject cataloging/classification.

University

	MEAN	FIRST QUARTILE	MEDIAN	THIRD QUARTILE
North Atlantic N=95 Range=$18,807-$67,700	33,668	28,575	32,000	36,000
Great Lakes & Plains N=133 Range=$21,000-$55,777	33,729	28,008	32,000	39,002
Southeast N=101 Range=$21,456-$42,841	28,679	25,784	27,550	31,392
West & Southwest N=123 Range=$21,080-$59,316	32,296	26,250	30,500	37,048
All Regions N=452 Range=$18,807-$67,700	32,198	26,825	30,824	35,808

All Academic and Public Libraries

	MEAN	FIRST QUARTILE	MEDIAN	THIRD QUARTILE
North Atlantic N=227 Range=$17,998-$67,700	34,103	28,000	32,246	38,608
Great Lakes & Plains N=243 Range=$17,826-$72,684	33,441	27,885	31,875	37,653
Southeast N=201 Range=$16,500-$52,815	28,970	25,000	27,405	32,651
West & Southwest N=240 Range=$18,500-$59,316	33,299	26,935	31,904	38,148
All Regions N=911 Range=$16,500-$72,684	32,582	26,740	31,010	37,107

18

SOURCE: ALA SURVEY OF LIBRARIAN SALARIES, 1993

Children's and/or Young Adult Services Librarian

Plans and conducts library services for children and/or young adults. Advises on reading materials. Selects materials for the collection. May plan and conduct special programs and outreach services.

Medium-sized Public Library
(Serving a population of from 25,000 to 99,999)

	MEAN	FIRST QUARTILE	MEDIAN	THIRD QUARTILE
North Atlantic N=72 Range=$20,248-$51,806	31,673	27,406	30,456	34,836
Great Lakes & Plains N=62 Range=$19,907-$53,427	30,128	25,704	28,771	33,322
Southeast N=20 Range=$19,000-$35,827	26,254	23,025	25,312	30,316
West & Southwest N=39 Range=$20,779-$49,944	34,081	27,330	32,712	40,500
All Regions N=193 Range=$19,000-$53,427	31,101	26,562	30,244	34,561

Large Public Library
(Serving a population of 100,000 or more)

	MEAN	FIRST QUARTILE	MEDIAN	THIRD QUARTILE
North Atlantic N=225 Range=$21,600-$54,783	34,988	28,979	33,374	39,065
Great Lakes & Plains N=229 Range=$22,572-$44,540	31,160	27,664	30,202	34,021
Southeast N=114 Range=$20,197-$43,308	29,854	25,454	28,289	33,900
West & Southwest N=224 Range=$20,340-$67,260	34,056	30,415	33,012	37,878
All Regions N=792 Range=$20,197-$67,260	32,879	28,476	31,476	36,919

SOURCE: ALA SURVEY OF LIBRARIAN SALARIES, 1993

Plans and conducts library services for children and/or young adults. Advises on reading materials. Selects materials for the collection. May plan and conduct special programs and outreach services.

All Public Libraries

	MEAN	FIRST QUARTILE	MEDIAN	THIRD QUARTILE
North Atlantic N=297 Range=$20,248-$54,783	34,185	28,800	32,883	38,379
Great Lakes & Plains N=291 Range=$19,907-$53,427	30,940	27,232	30,098	34,008
Southeast N=134 Range=$19,000-$43,308	29,317	25,275	27,800	33,504
West & Southwest N=263 Range=$20,340-$67,260	34,060	29,987	33,012	38,100
All Regions N=985 Range=$19,000-$67,260	32,530	27,800	31,333	36,715

SOURCE: ALA SURVEY OF LIBRARIAN SALARIES, 1993

Beginning Librarian
(Page 1 of 3)

Full-time staff member with a master's degree from a graduate library education program accredited by ALA, but no professional experience.

Medium-sized Public Library
(Serving a population of from 25,000 to 99,999)

	MEAN	FIRST QUARTILE	MEDIAN	THIRD QUARTILE
North Atlantic N=16 Range=$20,000-$30,811	25,840	24,386	25,578	27,897
Great Lakes & Plains N=8 Range=$16,000-$25,600	22,203	20,750	22,351	24,910
Southeast N=3 Range=$25,662-$26,954	26,523	25,662	26,954	26,954
West & Southwest N=6 Range=$17,000-$35,645	27,173	22,848	27,144	33,259
All Regions N=33 Range=$16,000-$35,645	25,263	22,701	25,092	26,954

Large Public Library
(Serving a population of 100,000 or more)

	MEAN	FIRST QUARTILE	MEDIAN	THIRD QUARTILE
North Atlantic N=64 Range=$21,000-$31,396	26,145	25,873	26,280	26,280
Great Lakes & Plains N=49 Range=$18,950-$30,615	25,126	23,467	25,935	26,074
Southeast N=45 Range=$20,000-$29,744	23,784	21,646	22,657	26,644
West & Southwest N=54 Range=$19,413-$38,736	26,531	22,339	27,071	30,744
All Regions N=212 Range=$18,950-$38,736	25,507	22,920	26,002	26,946

SOURCE: ALA SURVEY OF LIBRARIAN SALARIES, 1993

Full-time staff member with a master's degree from a graduate library education program accredited by ALA, but no professional experience.

Two-Year College

	MEAN	FIRST QUARTILE	MEDIAN	THIRD QUARTILE
North Atlantic N=4 Range=$21,000-$37,000	28,948	24,060	28,897	33,837
Great Lakes & Plains N=1 Range=$26,000-$26,000	26,000	26,000	26,000	26,000
Southeast N=4 Range=$24,000-$28,000	25,549	24,500	25,099	26,599
West & Southwest N=6 Range=$23,000-$44,400	32,867	28,000	31,951	37,897
All Regions N=15 Range=$21,000-$44,400	29,413	25,000	28,000	35,903

Four-Year College

	MEAN	FIRST QUARTILE	MEDIAN	THIRD QUARTILE
North Atlantic N=10 Range=$19,000-$26,500	23,220	22,000	22,900	25,700
Great Lakes & Plains N=4 Range=$19,709-$23,000	21,427	20,355	21,500	22,500
Southeast N=3 Range=$22,500-$25,080	23,860	22,500	24,000	25,080
West & Southwest N=5 Range=$19,500-$42,704	28,507	23,300	27,300	29,733
All Regions N=22 Range=$19,000-$42,704	24,183	22,000	23,150	25,700

SOURCE: ALA SURVEY OF LIBRARIAN SALARIES, 1993

Full-time staff member with a master's degree from a graduate library education program accredited by ALA, but no professional experience.

University

	MEAN	FIRST QUARTILE	MEDIAN	THIRD QUARTILE
North Atlantic N=32 Range=$21,000-$61,750	29,514	25,097	28,250	31,713
Great Lakes & Plains N=33 Range=$21,500-$28,980	25,225	24,000	25,331	25,825
Southeast N=30 Range=$19,764-$48,450	24,804	21,630	24,000	25,400
West & Southwest N=43 Range=$20,000-$38,800	25,061	22,596	23,595	26,500
All Regions N=138 Range=$19,764-$61,750	26,077	23,000	25,000	28,000

All Academic and Public Libraries

	MEAN	FIRST QUARTILE	MEDIAN	THIRD QUARTILE
North Atlantic N=126 Range=$19,000-$61,750	26,819	25,000	26,280	28,000
Great Lakes & Plains N=95 Range=$16,000-$30,615	24,768	23,459	25,331	26,060
Southeast N=85 Range=$19,764-$48,450	24,327	21,715	24,000	26,308
West & Southwest N=114 Range=$17,000-$44,400	26,431	22,680	24,877	30,359
All Regions N=420 Range=$16,000-$61,750	25,745	22,884	25,586	27,060

SOURCE: ALA SURVEY OF LIBRARIAN SALARIES, 1993

Discussion

Summary of Results

People interested in a particular type of library or a particular type of work, or a particular region will have their own way of drawing conclusions from the results of this survey. However, the results may be summarized in a very general way by observing mean salaries paid to particular positions, mean salaries paid by particular types of libraries, or mean salaries paid in particular parts of the U.S.

Salaries by Position

The six positions are shown in rank order by mean of salaries paid on Table 1. Two additional columns are also given: a column showing the dollar amount of change from 1992 to 1993 and a column indicating the percent of increase.

Table 1. Rank Order of Position Titles by Mean of Salaries Paid				
			Change	
Title	93 Salary	92 Salary	Amount	%
Director	53,331	51,326[1]	+2,005	+3.9
Deputy/Associate/Assistant Director	47,070	46,966	+104	+0.2
Department Head/Branch Head	39,352	39,017	+335	+0.9
Reference/Information Librarian	33,001	32,528	+473	+1.5
Cataloger and/or Classifier	32,582	32,746	-164	-0.5
Children's and/or Young Adult Services Librarian	32,530	33,242	-712	-2.1

SOURCE: ALA SURVEY OF LIBRARIAN SALARIES, 1993

1. This figure was incorrect on Table 1 in the 1992 report.

The average of the percent of increase over the past year is .7 percent if all six position titles are considered. It is 1.2 percent without the title of Children's and/or Young Adult Services Librarian, the position showing a very unusual percent increase from 1991 to 1992. In either case, the figure is much lower than the increase in comparable occupations reported by the U.S. Bureau of Labor Statistics (BLS) in the June 1993 *Monthly Labor Review*. A table entitled "Employment Cost Index, wages and salaries by occupation and industry group" shows that civilian workers consisting of private industry, state and local government, but excluding farm, household, and federal government workers, received an average 3.5 percent increase in 1992 over the previous year. White collar workers also received an average increase of 3.5 percent in 1992.

Table 2. Percent Change in Mean of Salaries Paid 1988-1993					
	88 to 89	89 to 90	90 to 91	91 to 92	92 to 93
Title	%	%	%	%	%
Director	+9	+2.0	+8.9	+6.0	+3.9
Deputy/Associate/Assistant Director	+14	+3.5	+8.9	+4.0	+0.2
Department Head/Branch Head	+12	+4.5	+7.8	+5.7	+0.9
Reference/Information Librarian	+9	+6.2	+5.1	+3.2	+1.5
Cataloger and/or Classifier	+13	+5.9	+5.2	+2.8	-0.5
Children's and/or Young Adult Services Librarian	+15	+6.4	+8.0	+11.3	-2.1

Table 2 shows the percent change in mean salaries for the six positions in each of the last 5 years. Two of the non-administrative positions show steady decline--Reference/Information Librarian and Cataloger and/or Classifier. The other positions are irregular but the trend is clear. Librarian salaries are increasing at a decreasing rate.

Salaries by Type of Library

When one considers salaries by type of library, it is useful to separate positions into three groups: the administrative positions found in all types of libraries (Director, Deputy/Associate/Assistant Director, Department Head/Branch Head); the other two positions found in all libraries (Reference/Information Librarian, Cataloger and/or Classifier); and the one position found only in public libraries (Children's and/or Young Adult Services Librarian).

The mean of salaries paid is highest in large public libraries for Director and for Deputy/Associate/Assistant Director and lowest for both in four-year colleges. For Department Head/Branch Head, the mean is highest in two-year colleges and lowest in medium-sized public libraries. For the other two common positions, the mean is always highest in two-year colleges, lowest in medium-sized public libraries for Cataloger and lowest in four-year colleges for Reference/Information Librarian. For the position found only in public libraries--Children's and/or Young Adult Services Librarian--the mean of salaries paid is higher in large public libraries.

Salaries by Region of the U.S.

In order to determine which region has the highest salaries, we analyzed the six positions and the five library size/type categories. When the region with the highest mean salary was marked for each position in each size/type category, North Atlantic was checked 51.8 percent of the time, West and Southwest was checked 40.7 percent of the time, Great Lakes and Plains was highest 7.4 percent of the time, and Southeast was never highest. This is the first time since our survey began that West and

Southwest has not had the largest percentage of highest mean salaries. The lowest mean salary was in the Southeast over 96 percent of the time. This pattern is similar to what has been observed in all previous surveys in this series.

Complicating Factors

When designing this survey over ten years ago, we were aware that several aspects of the patterns of employment in libraries would complicate our efforts. As we talked with respondents and users of the reports over the years, we gained additional insights into several factors which should be taken into consideration when using these results.

The Meaning of "Full-Time"

The questionnaire asked about salaries for **full-time** positions only, but full-time was not defined. There are at least two problems in this area: How many months in a year is full-time? How do you report people who work full-time in the library but part-time at one job and part-time at another?

The months in a year problem primarily affects academic libraries where librarians sometimes have academic year contracts for less than twelve months. In this survey, respondents are asked to indicate the number of months a salary covers and the computer calculated twelve months at the same rate. Appendix G shows how often less-than-twelve-month salaries occur.

Another complication related to the issue of "full-time" is the fact that one librarian may fill more than one position. For example: a public librarian may work part-time as a children's librarian and part-time as a cataloger; an academic librarian may be a reference librarian as well as a department head (of reference department). Survey instructions told the respondent:

> If a staff member works full-time but performs duties of more than one position, list him or her as incumbent in the position which you consider his or her major responsibility. **List each staff member only once.**

The Meaning of "Professional"

In the early years of this survey, respondents were asked to report only salaries paid to professionals, but the word "professional" was not defined. Instead, each position was described in such a way that professional responsibility was clearly implied. Instructions told the respondent to list all incumbents in these positions "regardless of academic credentials." We accepted the judgment of the respondent that the salaries reported were for professional work but found out, when we called about low salaries (see below), that some respondents had doubts about whether a particular incumbent could be described as "professional." When such doubts were expressed, we asked the respondent to make a decision based on the definition in ALA's statement on "Library Education and Personnel Utilization." (See Appendix B, Policy 54.1, Section 8.) In 1990, that definition was added to the instructions.

Beginning with the 1991 survey, we asked respondents to report only staff *with master's degrees from graduate library education programs accredited by ALA*. We know that many respondents paid attention to this instruction because questionnaires were returned to us with notes that no one in the library, or no one in a certain position, had the MLS. On the other hand, we also know that some did not follow instructions because of what we learned when calling about salaries below the cut off point (see below).

The questionnaire also requested another type of information which helped to ensure that only salaries for professional positions were included in this report. Following each position title and description was a line for "Position Title (if different from above)." When screening revealed such titles as "secretary," "library assistant" or "technical assistant" on that line, the salary information was not used.

Salaries Below $19,000

In previous years this report has described the methodology used to determine the cut-off point below which salaries were dropped as probably not being for full-time, professional work. The cut-off point for the 1993 survey was $19,000. Of the 11,096 salaries initially entered into the file, forty-three were below $19,000 (less than 1%). Staff at the Library Research Center conducted telephone interviews with directors at the twenty-nine libraries involved and learned that twenty of the forty-three salaries were for part-time work or were paid to staff without the specified degree. Those twenty salaries were dropped from the file used for the report. Another was corrected to be over $19,000. Once the twenty salaries were dropped the total was 11,076 salaries. The dropped salaries had been reported primarily because the respondent had misunderstood the instructions.

Twenty-two salaries of less than $19,000 did remain in the file. Fifteen were in a public library and seven were in an academic library.

Job Levels or Faculty Ranks

The wording of this questionnaire is based on an assumption that librarians are compensated at a particular amount for doing a particular job (e.g., reference). However, in many libraries that is not true. Some libraries use a system of levels in their compensation structure (e.g., Librarian I, II, III, IV) to account for the background a person brings to a job and the amount of responsibility it entails. Compensation is based on level, not on the type of work done as defined by our position descriptions. Some academic libraries pay salaries based on faculty rank rather than work done. In many academic libraries where librarians have faculty rank and titles, they are compensated as Instructor, Assistant Professor, Associate Professor or Professor and not as any one of the position titles on our questionnaire. We do not attempt to account for this variety within the structure of our questionnaire and every year some respondents tell us it was impossible to complete the questionnaire for this reason.

Several respondents and reviewers of this report have recommended in the past that we collect salary data for librarian levels or ranks. We have considered this seriously, but concluded that it would be at least as confusing as the current method due to the fact that levels and ranks mean different things in different libraries.

Longevity Pay

Some large public libraries were unable to report exact salaries for each position due to the large number of incumbents and the small amount of time available. In several such cases, respondents reported the number of incumbents for a position that were in a specific range on the salary schedule and we used the midpoint of that range for the appropriate number of incumbents. While reasonable in a national study that reports summary statistics, this procedure does not take into account longevity pay which is related to individual tenure and not to a point on the salary schedule. Thus some incumbents may be earning more than is reported here.

Level of Experience

Respondents occasionally ask us to ask for and report salaries in a way that takes into account the years of experience that an incumbent possesses. Unfortunately, providing that information would be a burden on respondents and reporting it would make this report overly complex. This report does take such factors into account in two ways: beginning librarian salaries are reported in a separate table and are not included in salary data for specific positions; and data for specific positions show figures at the first and third quartile as well as the mean, median, and range.

Salary Surveys Providing Information on Library Workers

Most library salary surveys listed below are conducted on a regular schedule (annual or biennial) and on a regional or national basis. The library literature should be monitored for reports of one-time surveys by individual libraries or associations. Some state library agencies collect salary and benefits data as part of their ongoing statistical gathering efforts from libraries within their own state. There is wide variation, however, in what data are collected and how these are compiled and reported. Most collect only public library data. Academic and school library data may be collected by other state agencies.

In addition, some state library associations collect salary data, issue recommended salary guidelines, set minimum salaries for professional positions, or publish reports in association journals or newsletters. As of June 1993, twenty states had established recommended minimum salaries. These include: Connecticut, Delaware, Illinois, Indiana, Iowa, Louisiana, Maine, Massachusetts, New Jersey, New York, North Carolina, Ohio, Pennsylvania, Rhode Island, South Carolina, South Dakota, Texas, Vermont, West Virginia, and Wisconsin. Specific amounts are not listed here because these are regularly updated by the associations. The latest figures can be found in the most recent classified section of *American Libraries* or *College & Research Libraries News*. A list of state library agency and association addresses can be found in *The Bowker Annual: Library and Book Trade Almanac*.

Individual libraries will sometimes conduct private surveys of institutions of comparable size or in the same geographical area, either through an outside consulting firm or by calling libraries informally. For the most part, these surveys are not published, although the initiating library will often share results with participating libraries. Some library workers are also conducting surveys that compare their salaries with other professions and occupations within their jurisdiction in an effort to achieve pay equity with positions requiring comparable skills, effort, responsibilities and working conditions.

Academic Libraries

Association of Research Libraries. *ARL Annual Salary Survey*. Washington, D.C.: ARL.

The annual survey shows the number of filled positions, average years of experience, and average, median and beginning salaries for professional positions in all ARL libraries. In addition, tables present the number of staff, average salaries, and years of experience for twenty-seven position categories and display findings on the present incumbents of these positions by sex and minority group membership, and by geographical location, size, and type of institution. Salaries for staff in law and medical libraries are presented in two separate series of tables. Salary data for staff in Canadian university libraries are also displayed in Canadian dollars.

Order from ARL, 21 DuPont Circle, NW, Suite 800, Washington, D.C. 20036, 202/296-2296. The 1992 survey, published in January 1993, is available for $20/ARL members or $60/non-members.

College and University Personnel Association. *1992-93 Administrative Compensation Survey Report.* Washington, D.C.: CUPA.

Annual survey; 1992-93 survey includes data on 167 college and university administrative positions from 1,432 public and private institutions. The tables in the survey present the median salary and salary percentiles according to institutional budget, enrollment and classification. Directors of library services are included, as well as circulation, acquisitions, reference, technical, and public services librarians.

The survey is available from CUPA, 1233 20th St., NW, Suite 503, Washington, D.C. 20036, 202/429-0311; $75 for association members, $175 for non-members/survey participants, and $295 for non-members/survey non-participants.

American Library Association. Association of College and Research Libraries. New England Chapter. *Salary Survey of New England College Libraries.*

The New England Chapter publishes this survey, begun in 1986-87, now biennially. Included are four year undergraduate institutions in the six New England states. Overall average, median and beginning salaries are given for individual institutions and average salaries are given for twenty four positions and by size of institution for four categories of staff. 1991-92 edition $5. Make check payable to ACRL/NEC Chapter. Contact Fay Zipkowitz, Associate Professor, GSLIS, University of Rhode Island, Kingston, RI 02881.

Public Libraries

American Library Association. Public Library Association. *Public Library Data Service Statistical Report.* Chicago: PLA.

Annual listing with information that includes library-specific salaries for directors and beginning librarians for most public libraries serving 100,000 or more and for many smaller libraries, as well as basic library statistics. (Replaces statistical reports of the Urban Libraries Council and the Allen County, Indiana biennial report of statistics of public libraries serving 100,000.) The 1993 edition is available from ALA Order Services, 50 E. Huron St., Chicago, IL 60611, 800/545-2433 ext. 5106 for $60 with the usual discounts for PLA and ALA members.

Lisa Guerreri. "Salaries of Municipal Officials for 1992" in *The Municipal Year Book,* 1993. Washington, D.C.: International City/County Management Association.

Chief librarian salaries for local public libraries are included with earnings of other city department heads. These are reported by geographic region, population size, city type (i.e., central, suburban, independent) and form of government. The mean, median, and first and third quartiles are included for libraries serving ten different population groups ranging from under 2,500 to over 1,000,000. *The Municipal Year Book* is usually published in April or May of each year and includes salary data for previous year. For details, contact Evelina Moulder, ICMA, 777 N. Capitol St., Suite 500, Washington, D.C. 20002, 202/289-4262.

Library salary data from the *Municipal Year Book* 1992 is summarized by Mary Jo Lynch and published in "Salaries of Library Directors," *Public Libraries* 31 (July/August 1992).

Sandstedt, Carl R. *Salary Survey: West-North-Central States.* St. Peters, Mo.: St. Charles City-County Library.

Annual survey provides data for directors, assistant directors, department heads, starting MLS, and several support positions for public libraries in West-North-Central States (North Dakota, South Dakota, Nebraska, Kansas, Minnesota, Iowa, Missouri). Average salaries are presented by size of library budget. Also includes per FTE costs, per capita support, and per capita materials budget.

Usually available in April for current calendar year. Send $5 for first copy, $2 per additional copy. Diskettes with .WKS files are $10. Please prepay. A $5 invoicing fee will be made for all orders requiring an invoice. Salary Survey, St. Charles City-County Library, 425 Spencer Rd., Box 529, St. Peters, MO 63376, 314/441-2300.

School Libraries

Educational Research Service, Inc. *National Survey of Salaries and Wages in Public Schools*. Arlington, Va.: ERS.

Since 1974-75, ERS has published an annual report of salaries for public school personnel, which includes data for school librarians and library clerks. Usually published in three volumes, the report covers scheduled salaries for professional personnel and actual salaries paid for professional and support personnel by enrollment group, per pupil expenditure, and geographic region.

The 1992-93 report costs $52 for each of the three volumes; available from ERS, 2000 Clarendon Blvd., Arlington, VA 22201, 703/243-2100.

Miller, Marilyn L., and Schontz, Marilyn. "Expenditures for Resources in School Library Media Centers," *School Library Journal*.

As part of a report every two years on budgets for and expenditures by school library media centers, some median and mean salary data for media specialists are reported by level of school. Included are comparisons of schools with and without district level library media coordinators. October 1993 issue will have the latest data.

National Education Association. *Estimates of School Statistics*. Washington, D.C.: NEA.

Annual statistical data for the fifty states and District of Columbia include estimated average annual salaries of total instructional staff and also separate data for classroom teachers by state and region. Librarian data are not given separately, however, but are grouped with teachers, principals, supervisors, guidance and psychological personnel and related instructional workers.

The annual compilation is usually available each spring. The 1992-93 report, published in 1993, is available for $14.95 for non-NEA members. Contact NEA Professional Library, PO Box 509, West Haven, CT 06516, 203/934-2669, 800-229-4200.

Special Libraries

American Association of Law Libraries. *Survey of Private Law Libraries*. Chicago: AALL in cooperation with SLA.

The survey provides compensation data for a variety of administrative and support staff positions and by functional areas, years of experience, budget range, and number of patrons served. Compensation is defined as salary as well as any cash bonuses received.

1991 survey report available for $70 from AALL, 53 W. Jackson Blvd., Suite 940, Chicago, IL 60604, 312/939-4764. Next survey is scheduled for 1993.

American Bar Association. *Statistical Survey of Law School Libraries and Librarians*. Office of Consultant on Legal Education.

Annual survey based on questionnaire by the American Bar Association to 176 law school libraries. Salary data are a small part of other statistics gathered. Includes median and average salaries of full time professional law librarians and support staff by school. Full report for $100 from the Assistant Consultant on Legal Education to the American Bar Association, c/o James P. White, Indiana University, 550 W. North Street, Indianapolis, IN 46202, 317/264-8350.

Art Libraries Society of North America. *ARLIS/NA Salary Survey, 1990*. Tucson, Ariz.: ARLIS/NA, 1991.

First salary survey of ARLIS/NA members provides information separately for those who spend 50 percent or more of their time with visual resources (e.g., slides, photographs, film, video) and those who work primarily with textual materials. Data were analyzed in relation to several variables (region, type of parent institution, library degree and arts degree). Full, 32-page report available for $10 prepaid from ARLIS/NA, 3900 E. Timrod St., Tucson, AZ 85711, 602/881-8479. Summary report in *Art Documentation* 11:93-94 (Summer 1992).

Association of Academic Health Sciences Library Directors. *Annual Statistics of Medical School Libraries in the United States and Canada*. Houston, Texas.

Salaries are provided for director, associate director, division head, department head, other librarians, and entry level positions. Minimum, maximum, and mean are provided for the positions and arranged by region.

Salary data for 1992-93 are included in the 15th edition. It is available at a cost of $50 for members of the Association of Academic Health Sciences Library Directors and $100 for non-members. This edition and previous editions may be ordered by contacting Sandra Wilson, AAHSLD, 1133 M.D. Anderson Blvd., Houston, TX 77030, 713/790-7060.

Medical Library Association. *MLA Salary Survey*. Chicago: MLA.

Triennial survey data cover geographic area, position level, type of institution, years of experience, education, primary area of responsibility, benefits, and other information.

The 1992 MLA member salary survey is available at a cost of $26 for members; $52 for non-members from MLA, 6 N. Michigan Ave., Suite 300, Chicago, IL 60602, 312/419-9094.

Special Libraries Association. *SLA Biennial Salary Survey*. Washington, D.C.: SLA.

Since 1967, SLA conducted an in-depth salary survey of members every three years. As of 1990, the in-depth survey is conducted every two years. Results are now issued as separate publications. Salaries are reported at the 25th, 50th (median) and 75th percentiles and contain breakdowns by industry, geographic region, administrative responsibility, sex, education level, and experience. Data for the U.S. and Canada are presented in separate tables. Annual updates, using a random sampling of 25 percent of the membership and an abbreviated questionnaire, were started in 1977 and are used in years between the now biennial surveys. The results of the updates are published in *Special Libraries* in the fall issue.

The survey data collected in 1990 were published in 1991; the report sells for $30 (members); $37.50 (non-members). Contact Special Libraries Association, 1700 18th St., N.W., Washington, D.C. 20009, 202/234-4700.

State Library Agencies

Council of State Governments. "COSLA/CSG Survey--Table 1 - Salary Data: State Library Agencies." Lexington, KY.: CSG.

The annual survey of salary data for state library agencies compiled earlier by the Association of Specialized and Cooperative Library Agencies now is carried out by the Council of State Governments for the Chief Officers of State Library Agencies (COSLA). Included is information on the salary for each state for a variety of positions: state librarian, assistant director, director of library operations or library services, director of library development or networking, FSCS data coordinator, consultants, specialists, and beginning professionals.

To order, contact Angela Crouch, Council of State Governments, Center for Management and Administration, Ironworks Pike, PO Box 11910, Lexington, KY 40578, 606/231-1925.

Other

Association for Library and Information Science Education. *Library and Information Science Education Statistical Report*. Raleigh, NC.: ALISE, 1980-.

Average and median salaries for faculty and administrators in ALISE member schools are provided in this annual report by sex, rank, and term of appointment.

Back issues (1981-) of the report are available from ALISE, 4101 Lake Boone Trail, Suite 201, Raleigh, NC 27607, 919/787-5181 for $15 each plus postage and handling: $4. Current issue is $30 plus postage and handling (U.S. funds). Annual report usually published in the summer.

College and University Personnel Association. *1992-93 National Faculty Salary Survey by Discipline and Rank in State Colleges and Universities*. Washington, D.C.: CUPA.

College and University Personnel Association. *1992-93 National Faculty Salary Survey by Discipline and Rank in Private Colleges and Universities.* Washington, D.C.: CUPA.

Annual surveys collect data for five faculty ranks in fifty-five disciplines and major fields. A total of 269 state and 487 private institutions participated in the most recent study. Communications, Communication Technologies, Computer Information Sciences, and Library and Archival Sciences are included. The listings are for those who teach in library science programs, not those who hold faculty rank as academic librarians. Faculty Salary Surveys are each $30 for survey participants, $50 for CUPA members/survey non-participants and $75 for non-members/survey non-participants from CUPA, 1233 20th St., NW, Suite 301, Washington, D.C. 20036, 202/429-0311.

Zipkowitz, Fay. "Placements and Salaries." *Library Journal.* Annual.

Annual survey since 1951 of recent graduates of ALA-accredited library education programs (usually published in a fall issue of *Library Journal* with data from previous calendar year). For each reporting school, the low, high, average, and median salaries are reported for men, women, and total placements. This information is also provided for five regions of the U.S. An additional table shows the distribution of high, low, average, and median salaries by type of library for men and women. The latest listing, "Placements and Salaries 1992" will be published in *Library Journal*, October 15, 1993. Canadian schools are no longer included.

Employee Benefits

Although some states collect data on employee benefits, little information is collected on a regional or national level on a regular basis for library workers.

PROVIDENCE Associates, Inc. *Public Library Work Benefits Survey.* Denton, Tex.: 1993.

Results of a survey of seventy-five public libraries in 1993 provides salary ranges and average salaries for five staff levels, plus data on vacation days, holidays, sick leave, leave of absence, pension plans, health and life insurance, and other benefits. Single copies available for $27.50 plus $2.50 postage/handling, from PROVIDENCE Associates, Inc., 419 S. Carroll Blvd. 2A, Denton, TX 76201-5928, 817/566-0417.

American Library Association. Office for Library Personnel Resources. "Library Employee Benefits." Chicago. ALA, 1991.

Results of informal survey of public and academic library personnel directors and administrators regarding employee benefits. Summary report in *Library Personnel News*, vol. 5, no. 4, July-August 1991.

Salary Surveys for Other Library Workers and Related Information Professionals

For salary data on support staff or professional/specialist positions other than librarians, the following surveys are suggested as a start.

"Library Support Staff Salary Survey 1990" by Ed Martinez and Raymond Roney was published in *Library Mosaics*, July/August 1991, pp. 8-12 and reports on salaries by type of library (public, special, academic), four regions of the U.S., and the staff classifications of clerk, assistant, technician, and other non-master's degree positions.

U.S. Department of Labor, Bureau of Labor Statistics *Area Wage Surveys*. Each year surveys are done in over seventy standard metropolitan areas. The surveys concentrate on clerical and manual labor occupations; however, these will be useful as a source of pay data for clerical positions. Specifies average workweek and mean, median, and middle pay rates, as well as vacation benefits, insurance and pension plans, and shift differential information.

The Bureau also publishes annual surveys of professional, administrative, technical, and clerical positions. Primary fields covered are accounting, law, personnel management, engineering, chemistry, retail, clerical supervisory, drafting, and clerical. These surveys may provide useful data on non-librarian professional or specialist positions and on clerical positions. A subject bibliography on "Prices, Wages, and the Cost of Living" (SB.226) is available from GPO and gives order information for the area wage surveys and other publications on compensation.

State employment agencies also collect and publish some wage data.

Abbott, Langer and Associates, 548 First St., Crete, IL 60417 conducts annual salary surveys for the following fields: legal and related jobs in business and industry; industrial engineers; plant engineers; consulting engineering firms; service department; nonprofit organizations; research and development; manufacturing; security/loss prevention; MIS/data processing; accounting/financial jobs; sales/marketing management; personnel/industrial relations; and inter-city wage and salary differentials.

The *Compensation in Nonprofit Organizations* report contains information on salaries of Directors of Information with this type of employer. Mean, median, 1st & 3rd quartile, and 1st & 9th decile data, salary ranges, current salaries, and total compensation (salaries plus bonuses) are reported by supervisory responsibility, type of nonprofit organization, total annual budget, geographic scope of organization, number of employees, region, state, and metropolitan area.

Annotations of over 1,200 salary surveys, both domestic and foreign, can be found in *Available Pay Survey Reports: An Annotated Bibliography* (4th ed.) by Dr. Steven Langer (1993). Annotations are indexed by source, geographic area, type of employer, and job title/function/college curricula. (Available from Abbott, Langer & Associates, 548 First St., Crete, IL 60417.)

Datamation publishes an annual salary survey of computer and information systems personnel. The 1993 report is in the August 15, 1993 issue. This reports on average salaries for positions in systems analysis, programming, database administration, data entry, office automation, and computer operations, by industry and regions.

The *Public Relations Journal* publishes an annual survey of public relations personnel in its July issue.

ALA Policies Relating to Salary Issues

The following are policies endorsed by the ALA Council and included in the "ALA Policy Manual" which appears annually in the *ALA Handbook of Organization*.

Policy #54.1 Library Education and Personnel Utilization

Sec. 8 The title "Librarian" carries with it the connotation of "professional" in the sense that professional tasks are those which require a special background and education on the basis of which library needs are identified, problems are analyzed, goals are set, and original and creative solutions are formulated for them, integrating theory into practice, and planning, organizing, communicating, and administering successful programs of service to users of the library's materials and services. In defining services to users, the professional person recognizes potential users as well as current ones, and designs services which will reach all who could benefit from them.

Sec. 9 The title "Librarian" therefore should be used only to designate positions in libraries which utilize the qualifications and impose the responsibilities suggested above. Positions which are primarily devoted to the routine application of established rules and techniques, however useful and essential to the effective operation of a library's ongoing services, should not carry the word "Librarian" in the job title.

Sec. 11 The salaries for each (personnel) category should offer a range of promotional steps sufficient to permit a career-in-rank. The top salary in any category should overlap the beginning salary in the next higher category, in order to give recognition to the value of experience and knowledge gained on the job.

Sec. 19 Administrative responsibilities entail advanced knowledge and skills comparable to those represented by any other high-level specialty, and appointment to positions in top administration should normally require the qualifications of a Senior Librarian with a specialization in administration. This category, however, is not limited to administrators, whose specialty is only one of several specializations of value to the library service. There are many areas of special knowledge within librarianship which are equally important and to which equal recognition in prestige and salary should be given. Highly qualified persons with specialist responsibilities in some aspects of librarianship--archives, bibliography, reference, for example--should be eligible for advanced status and financial rewards without being forced to abandon for administrative responsibilities their areas of major competence.

Policy #54.4 Comparable Rewards

The American Library Association supports salary administration which gives reasonable and comparable recognition to positions having administrative, technical, subject, and linguistic requirements. It is recognized that all such specialist competencies can be intellectually vigorous and meet demanding professional operational needs. In administering such a policy, it can be a useful guide that, in major libraries, as many nonadministrative specialities be assigned to the top classifications as are administrative staff. Whenever possible there should be as many at the top rank with less than 30 percent administrative load as there are at the highest rank carrying over 70 percent administrative load.

Policy #54.7 Security of Employment for Library Employees

Security of employment, as an elementary right, guarantees specifically.....a sufficient degree of economic security to make employment in the library attractive to men and women of ability.

Policy #54.8 The Library's Pay Plan

Libraries should have a well-constructed and well-administered pay plan based on systematic analysis and evaluation of jobs in the library and which will assure equal pay for equal work. (Note: For text of full statement, see section following listing of policies.)

Policy #54.9 Permanent Part-Time Employment

The right to earn a living includes a right to part-time employment on a par with full-time employment, including prorated pay and fringe benefits, opportunity for advancement and protection of tenure, access to middle and upper level jobs, and exercise of full responsibilities at any level.

ALA shall create more voluntarily chosen upgraded permanent part-time jobs in its own organization and supports similar action on the part of all libraries.

Policy #54.10 Equal Opportunity and Salaries

The American Library Association supports and works for the achievement of equal salaries and opportunity for employment and promotion for men and women.

The Association fully supports the concept of comparable wages for comparable work that aims at levels of pay for female-oriented occupations equal to those of male-oriented occupations; ALA therefore supports all legal and legislative efforts to achieve wages for library workers commensurate with wages in other occupations with similar qualifications, training, and responsibilities.

ALA particularly supports the efforts of those library workers who have documented, and are legally challenging, the practice of discriminatory salaries, and whose success will benefit all library workers throughout the nation.

Policy #54.11 Collective Bargaining

The American Library Association recognizes the principle of collective bargaining as one of the methods of conducting labor-management relations used by private and public institutions. The Association affirms the right of eligible library employees to organize and bargain collectively with their employers, or to refrain from organizing and bargaining collectively, without fear of reprisal.

Policy #54.18 Advertising Salary Ranges

Available ranges shall be given for positions listed in any placement services provided by ALA and its units. A regional salary guide delineating the latest minimum salary figures recommended by state library associations shall be made available from any placement services provided by ALA and its units.

All ALA and unit publications printing classified job advertisements shall list the salary ranges established for open positions where available and shall include a regional salary guide delineating the latest minimum salary figures recommended by state library associations for library positions.

Full Text of Policy # 54.8: The Library's Pay Plan*

The American Library Association believes that an important factor in establishing and maintaining good library service is adequate pay for library employees as exemplified in a well-constructed and well-administered pay plan. A knowledge of the principles on which sound salary administration is based must be the foundation of an equitable pay plan. To aid the library's governing board, its administration, and its staff in the formulation, promulgation, and operation of such a pay plan, the ALA Board on Personnel Administration sets forth in a series of related statements the principles of salary planning and administration.

1. A sound pay plan will be predicated on a systematic analysis and evaluation of jobs in the library, and will reflect the current organization and objectives of the library, recognizing different levels of difficulty and responsibility inherent in various positions, whether these are classified as professional, nonprofessional, administrative, specialist, maintenance, or trade; the relationship among positions in terms of difficulty and responsibility will thus be expressed in a unified plan which will integrate all types of service and will assure equal pay for equal work.

2. An equitable salary schedule will be provided for each class of position which is comparable to that received by persons employed in analogous work in the area and required to have analogous training and qualifications.

   The salaries of nonprofessional employees, maintenance and skilled trade workers employed by the library system will compare with those of local workers performing similar duties. The salary schedules for professional library positions, in the case of the community where the pay scale does not meet competing rates outside, may need to exceed the prevailing local level for other professional personnel. Since the recruiting of professionally trained librarians is on a nation-wide basis, the library system must compete with rates paid in the country as a whole in order to obtain and retain a high quality of professional personnel. In libraries in educational institutions (elementary, secondary, and higher education) the professional librarians will normally be on the faculty pay plan, with the salary schedules of the various classes of faculty rank adjusted to compensate equitably for such factors as shorter vacations and longer work week; where a separate pay plan is used, it will be comparable with that of the faculty and adjusted to compensate equitably for such factors as vacation and work week.

3. An equitable salary schedule will provide for each class of position a minimum and a maximum salary and a series of increments within each salary range, such increments to be granted on the basis of demonstrated competence, individual development (whether through growth on the job or through formal education), and attitude.

---

*Note: This policy was passed by the ALA Council in July 1955. It still remains a useful statement regarding the administration of a library's pay plan. Readers should note, however, that the references to the Board on Personnel Administration are not applicable since this unit is no longer in existence.

4. The library system in developing a pay plan, and in reviewing it to maintain its adequacy, will identify one or more key positions in the professional and in the other services, set salary schedules for these positions which are comparable to prevailing rates for such positions, and develop and adjust the salary schedule for other levels of positions in relation to the salary schedules set for each of these key positions.

5. The pay plan ladder consisting of the salary schedules for the various classes of positions will provide an orderly progression from the lowest to the highest schedule, with each schedule reflecting properly the difference in level of duties and responsibilities of positions in that classification from those in the schedule below and above it but without wide gaps or serious overlapping between schedules.

6. An equitable pay plan will reflect living costs in the community, the cost of maintaining an appropriate level of living, and the ability of the jurisdiction to pay for the service.

7. All policies and rules concerning the operation and administration of the pay plan will be set forth clearly in writing and will accompany the pay plan.

8. Though final approval and adoption of the pay plan and rules for its operation rest with the governing board and administration of the library, it is desirable that the library staff participates in the formulation of both the plan and its operating rules.

9. Each staff member will be informed of the salary schedule for his or her class of position, of the relation of that schedule to the pay plan as a whole, and of the policies and rules governing the operation of the plan.

The current studies of the ALA Board on Personnel Administration giving salary data for key positions will provide useful material for the library system in developing and maintaining the adequacy of its pay plan.

Selected Bibliography on Compensation and Employee Benefits

Compiled by the
ALA Office for Library Personnel Resources

Note: The earlier editions of *ALA Survey of Librarian Salaries* contained selected citations on compensation that readers may wish to consult since many of these references are still useful. Items listed below have been published since the previous listings were compiled.

Bartol, Kathryn M. and Laura L. Hagmann. "Team-Based Pay Plans: A Key to Effective Teamwork." *Compensation and Benefits Review* 24:24-29 (November/December 1992).

Bunning, Richard L. "Models for Skill-Based Pay Plans." *HRMagazine* 37:62-64 (February 1992).

Burns, Kyle C. "A Bonus Plan that Promotes Customer Service." *Compensation and Benefits Review* 24:15-20 (September/October 1992).

Dolmat-Connell, Jack and Ken Cardinal. "Beyond Total Compensation: The Total-Cost Perspective." *Compensation and Benefits Review* 24:56-60 (January/February 1992).

England, Paula. *Comparable Worth. Theories and Evidence.* Hawthorne, N.Y.: Aldine de Gruyter, 1992.

Gray, Mary W. "Pay Equity Through Job Evaluation: A Case Study." *Compensation and Benefits Review* 24:46-51 (July/August 1992).

"How to Come Out on Top in a Job Classification Study." *Library Personnel News* 7:4 (January/February 1993).

Lawler, Edward E., Gerald E. Ledford, Jr., and Lei Chang. "Who Uses Skill-Based Pay, and Why." *Compensation and Benefits Review* 25:22-26 (March/April 1993).

Manicatide, Mircea and Virginia Pennell. "Key Developments in Compensation Management." *HRFocus* 69:3-4 (October 1992).

McConkey, Joan, et al. "Salary Equity: A Case Study." *College and Research Libraries* 54:33-41 (January 1993).

Milkovich, George and Carolyn Milkovich. "Strengthening the Pay-Performance Relationship: The Research." *Compensation and Benefits Review* 24:53-62 (November/December 1992).

"New Ideas in Compensation." *Library Personnel News* 7:5 (January/February 1993).

Newman, Jerry M. and Daniel J. Fisher. "Strategic Impact Merit Pay." *Compensation and Benefits Review* 24:38-45 (July/August 1992).

"Parallel Career Paths: Will They Work in Libraries." *Library Personnel News* 7:1,3-4 (January/ February 1993).

Schuster, Jay. R. and Patricia K. Zingheim. "The New Variable Pay: Key Design Issues." 25:27-34 (March/April 1993).

Toller, John M., et al. *1992 Survey of Compensation Practices in Higher Education*. Washington, D.C.: College and University Personnel Association, 1993.

Watkins, Bonnie with Jan Feye-Stukas. *Pay Equity & Minnesota Libraries: Results of a Legislative Approach*. Chicago: American Library Association Office for Library Personnel Resources, 1992.

Zipkowitz, Fay. "Jobs Tight, Salaries Holding." *Library Journal* 117:31-36 (October 15, 1992).

Technical Considerations

Formation of Library Groups

As in previous years, the survey samples were selected from two library universes--public and academic. The public library universe included all public libraries serving populations of 25,000 or more and was stratified into two classes--those serving populations of from 25,000 to 99,999 and those serving populations of 100,000 or more.

The academic library universe was stratified into three classes: two-year college, four-year college, and university. This stratification was based on the "Highest Offering" code used in the *1993 Directory of Higher Education* published by Higher Education Publications, Inc. The first of these three classes include schools that offer "two but less than four years." The second includes schools that offer a "four or five year baccalaureate." The third combines four categories: "first professional degree," "master's," "beyond master's but less than doctorate," "doctorate."

Within each of these five strata, libraries were further stratified into four geographic areas used frequently by National Center for Education Statistics (NCES): North Atlantic, Great Lakes and Plains, Southeast, and West and Southwest. A list of states included in each region is provided in Table D-1. As in previous surveys, the five library classes and four geographic areas were combined to form twenty groups from which samples were selected. Tables D2-D7 show the size of each group, the size of the sample, and the size of the return.

Sample Selection and Return

The size of the sample for each type/size/geographic strata was determined by using a proportional sampling procedure that took into account the size of the population in each group and the expected return rate for the survey. As in 1992, the public library sample was selected using a diskette from the NCES containing data on all public libraries submitted to NCES by state library agencies as part of the Federal State Cooperative System for Public Library Data (FSCS). This file includes data on the number of staff with master's degrees from graduate library education programs accredited by ALA. Before selecting the sample in 1993, we dropped from the sampling frame libraries that did not have at least two of such personnel. Because of this change in sampling frame, the numbers for size of group in Tables D2 and D3 are different from those in similar tables in the 1992 report. Once the sampling frame was established, the sample was drawn by strata as described above.

The procedure for selecting the academic library sample was also changed this year. Instead of using two tapes from NCES plus a diskette from the Carnegie Corporation for the Advancement of Teaching as in former years, we obtained a customized sampling frame from John Minter Associates based on the *1993 Higher Education Directory* and a tape from NCES on "Academic Libraries, 1990." Minter screened out several sets of institutions in the library from the full universe. Removed were institutions with fewer than two full-time professionals and institutions categorized as "specialized" by the Carnegie Corporation for the Advancement of Teaching. Those institutions offer degrees ranging from the bachelor's to the doctorate, at least 50 percent of which are in a single specialized field, e.g., "theological seminaries, Bible colleges, and other institutions offering degrees in religion," and "Schools of art, music, and design." Specialized institutions often declined to respond in the early years of this survey. Also excluded were four sets of institutions whose individual members had been unable to respond in the past. In New York, the seventeen institutions that are part of the City University of New York were removed because librarians there have full academic status and salary is not related to position description. Public two-year schools in California were removed for the same reason as were the fourteen members of the state university system in Pennsylvania. Also in Pennsylvania, we removed all but the main campus of Pennsylvania State University because librarians at other campuses declined to respond in the past and referred us to the main campus. The remaining institutions were sampled using the stratification plan described above. Finally, the preliminary sample was screened for libraries that refused to respond in 1990, 1991, or 1992 for reasons that seemed unlikely to change. Five such libraries were dropped from the sample.

In addition to the 946 returns analyzed for this report, we also received 20 returns that could not be used. They fell into the following categories:

- eight were simply blank

- two were from respondents in libraries where none of the full-time staff had master's degrees from graduate library education programs accredited by ALA.

- seven were refusals. Four were from public libraries and three from academic libraries. In all three of those cases, the institution's policy prohibits release of salary data.

- three were unuseable for miscellaneous reasons.

Procedure

The questionnaire and cover letter were mailed on March 31, 1993. A postage-paid business reply envelope was enclosed to encourage response. A second mailing was sent to all non-respondents in April. A third mailing was sent in May only to non-respondents in several strata where response was under 70 percent.

After questionnaires were screened at ALA, they were sent to the Library Research Center (LRC) of the University of Illinois Graduate School of Library and Information Science, where they were edited, entered into a microcomputer file, and analyzed using SPSS/PC+ (the microcomputer version of the Statistical Package for the Social Sciences).

Again this year a special procedure was followed for libraries that are members of the Association of Research Libraries. ARL, which includes about 100 of the largest university libraries in the U.S., conducts its own annual salary survey. Data are gathered for salaries as of July 1 and published the following spring. ARL libraries are also included in the sample for the ALA survey. In the past, some have declined to answer because they are unable to spend time completing another salary questionnaire. For the 1993 survey, ARL again agreed to cooperate with us to save work for everyone. After the sample was selected, we identified the ARL libraries on the list and sent the directors a special mailing asking them to release salaries already on file with ARL. All but five of the thirty ARL libraries in the sample agreed to release data. We sent ARL a list of the ARL position codes that matched the position descriptions in our questionnaire and ARL sent us a printout of salaries for those positions in the selected institutions. These salaries were entered into the data file along with salaries from other libraries.

This procedure worked well and saved time both in the libraries involved and in survey processing. It has two drawbacks, however. ARL salary figures are as of July 1992 whereas others are as of the following April. Thus, the figures for salaries in the university category in our report may be lower than what was paid in April 1993. Also, ARL does not specify that salaries should be reported only for staff with master's degrees from graduate library education programs accredited by ALA and ARL does include "other professionals" as well as librarians. For the most part, however, we expect that those "other professionals" are in the ARL position code of "Functional Specialist" which was *not* on the list of codes we requested from ARL. On balance, we believe this procedure had more benefits than drawbacks and intend to continue it as long as ARL is willing to cooperate.

Table D-1. States In Four Regions of the U.S.

NORTH ATLANTIC	GREAT LAKES AND PLAINS	SOUTHEAST	WEST AND SOUTHWEST
Connecticut	Illinois	Alabama	Alaska
Delaware	Indiana	Arkansas	Arizona
District of Columbia	Iowa	Florida	California
Maine	Kansas	Georgia	Colorado
Maryland	Michigan	Kentucky	Hawaii
Massachusetts	Minnesota	Louisiana	Idaho
New Hampshire	Missouri	Mississippi	Montana
New Jersey	Nebraska	North Carolina	Nevada
New York	North Dakota	South Carolina	New Mexico
Pennsylvania	Ohio	Tennessee	Oklahoma
Rhode Island	South Dakota	Virginia	Oregon
Vermont	Wisconsin	West Virginia	Texas
			Utah
			Washington
			Wyoming

Source: *Statistics of Public Libraries, 1977-78* (NCES, 1982)

Table D-2. Medium-Sized Public Libraries: Size of Group, Sample, Return

	GROUP	SAMPLE		RETURN	
	#	#	% of Group	#	% of Sample
North Atlantic	305	113	37.0	85	75.2
Great Lakes & Plains	277	103	37.2	80	77.7
Southeast	168	62	36.9	54	87.1
West and Southwest	178	66	37.1	48	72.7
TOTAL	928	344	37.1	267	77.6

Table D-3. Large Public Libraries: Size of Group, Sample, Return

	GROUP	SAMPLE		RETURN	
	#	#	% of Group	#	% of Sample
North Atlantic	82	46	56.1	35	76.1
Great Lakes & Plains	90	45	50.0	38	84.4
Southeast	129	56	43.4	47	83.9
West and Southwest	135	67	49.6	56	83.6
TOTAL	436	214	49.1	176	82.2

Table D-4. Two-Year College Libraries: Size of Group, Sample, Return

	GROUP	SAMPLE		RETURN	
	#	#	% of Group	#	% of Sample
North Atlantic	124	46	37.1	33	71.7
Great Lakes & Plains	113	46	40.7	31	67.4
Southeast	178	64	36.0	44	68.8
West and Southwest	123	46	37.4	34	73.9
TOTAL	538	202	37.5	142	70.3

Table D-5. Four-Year College Libraries: Size of Group, Sample, Return

	GROUP	SAMPLE		RETURN	
	#	#	% of Group	#	% of Sample
North Atlantic	93	45	48.4	32	71.1
Great Lakes & Plains	117	45	38.5	31	68.9
Southeast	115	46	40.0	32	69.6
West and Southwest	36	33	91.7	26	78.8
TOTAL	361	169	46.8	121	71.6

Table D-6. University Libraries: Size of Group, Sample, Return

	GROUP	SAMPLE		RETURN	
	#	#	% of Group	#	% of Sample
North Atlantic	240	86	35.8	63	73.3
Great Lakes & Plains	221	80	36.2	65	81.3
Southeast	199	73	36.7	55	75.3
West and Southwest	204	75	36.8	57	76.0
TOTAL	864	314	36.3	240	76.4

Table D-7. All Libraries Surveyed: Size of Group, Sample, Return

	GROUP	SAMPLE		RETURN	
	#	#	% of Group	#	% of Sample
North Atlantic	844	336	39.8	248	73.8
Great Lakes & Plains	818	319	39.0	245	76.8
Southeast	789	301	38.1	232	77.1
West and Southwest	676	287	42.5	221	77.0
TOTAL	3,127	1,243	39.8	946	76.1

49

AMERICAN LIBRARY ASSOCIATION

50 EAST HURON STREET   CHICAGO, ILLINOIS 60611-2795   U.S.A.
312-944-6780   800-545-2433
TELEX: 4909992000 ALA UI FAX: 312-440-9374   TDD: 312-944-7298

March 31, 1993

Dear Colleague:

ALA needs your help in providing information to the library community regarding salaries paid to librarians with master's degrees from programs accredited by ALA who hold full-time positions in academic and public libraries. Your institution has been selected as part of a random sample of libraries to whom the enclosed questionnaire has been sent. Only summary results will be reported; individual responses will not be identified.

ALA collected and published similar information biennially from 1982 to 1988, and annually since 1989. The results of these surveys have been useful to many people in the library community who need to know what salary might be paid to someone in a particular type of library position or in a particular geographical area. This information is useful to librarians applying for positions, to librarians setting salaries, and to many others interested in the compensation of librarians.

Because your library is one of a scientifically selected sample, your response is essential to the success of the survey. As an indication of our thanks for your help, all participants are entitled to a 25% discount on the price of the report. (Mention this entitlement when you place an order. The report will be published in September, 1993.) If your staff is very large and this form is difficult to use, please contact Mary Jo Lynch at the numbers given below. We want your response and will try to work with whatever data you can provide.

Please complete the enclosed questionnaire and return it in the enclosed self-addressed, postage-paid envelope. Please return it as soon as possible, but no later than **April 16, 1993**. If you have questions about the survey, please contact Mary Jo Lynch, Director, ALA Office for Research and Statistics at 1-800-545-2433, extension 4273, UØ8774@UICVM (Bitnet), or UØ8774@.UICVM.UIC.EDU (Internet).

Sincerely yours,

Peggy Sullivan
Executive Director
American Library Association

PS/srg

Enclosures (2)

P.S. Please help our budget by returning this form promptly. In order to ensure the validity of the results, reminders will be sent to nonrespondents. However, we would rather spend the postage money on other services.

AMERICAN LIBRARY ASSOCIATION SURVEY OF LIBRARIAN SALARIES, 1993

PART I. SALARIES PAID TO BEGINNING LIBRARIANS

A. Within the last 12 months has the library hired any full-time staff with master's degrees from graduate library education programs accredited by ALA but no professional experience? Circle one

No (if so, skip to Part II)   1
Yes   2

B. What is the annual salary paid such staff? Please list all annual salaries below as of April 1, 1993. **Do not repeat salaries of these librarians in Part II.** NOTE FOR ACADEMIC LIBRARIES: If the incumbent works LESS than a 12-month year (including vacation), please report the salary and circle the appropriate number of months (9 or 10) for which the salary is paid.

Annual Salary	Annual Salary	Annual Salary	Annual Salary
1 _____ 9 10	3 _____ 9 10	5 _____ 9 10	7 _____ 9 10
2 _____ 9 10	4 _____ 9 10	6 _____ 9 10	8 _____ 9 10

PART II. SALARIES PAID TO LIBRARIANS IN SELECTED POSITIONS

This section of the questionnaire requests information on annual salaries for selected positions ordinarily held by full-time staff with master's degrees from graduate library education programs accredited by ALA.

We realize that many libraries have positions that are not included in the questionnaire. **Do not include salaries for those positions.** Libraries may also fill the positions listed here with staff who have credentials other than master's degrees from graduate library education programs accredited by ALA. **Do not include salaries for those staff. Also, do not include salaries for part-time or support staff.**

Each page in Part II contains descriptions of several specific library positions. If your library has one or more staff with the specified degree employed **FULL-TIME** whose major responsibilities are covered by the position description, please provide the information requested on the form unless the salary was listed above in Part I, B. If a staff member works full-time but performs duties of more than one position, list him or her as incumbent in the position that you consider his or her major responsibility. **List each staff member only once** and give the full salary paid to the person. All **FULL-TIME** incumbents in these positions should be included regardless of the number of months worked in a year.* NOTE FOR ACADEMIC LIBRARIES: If the incumbent is considered full-time but works LESS than a 12-month year (including vacation), please report the salary and circle the appropriate number of months (9 or 10) for which the salary is paid.

For each position in which you have staff with master's degrees from graduate library education programs accredited by ALA employed **FULL-TIME**, please provide the annual salary of each incumbent as of April 1, 1993 except for the beginning librarians reported in Part I, B. Give actual dollars paid. Do not include fringe benefits. If you need additional space, please use separate sheets of paper or attach a computer printout.

*If services are contributed (i.e., institution pays some expenses or an honorarium but not a true salary), please do not list the incumbent.

POSITION TITLE: *Director* *

POSITION DESCRIPTION: Chief administrative officer of the library or library system. Plans and directs all aspects of the operation. May have job title such as Librarian or Head Librarian.

POSITION TITLE: *(if different from above)* _____

ANNUAL SALARY _____ 9 / 10   *Note for academic libraries: Circle 9 or 10 as appropriate if salary is for LESS than a 12 month year (including vacation).*

POSITION TITLE: *Deputy/Associate/Assistant Director* *

POSITION DESCRIPTION: Aids Director in planning and directing some or all aspects of library or library system. May manage a major aspect of the library operation (e.g., technical services, public services, collection development, systems/automation).

POSITION TITLE: *(if different from above)* _____

Annual Salary	Annual Salary	Annual Salary	Annual Salary
1 _____ 9/10	3 _____ 9/10	5 _____ 9/10	7 _____ 9/10
2 _____ 9/10	4 _____ 9/10	6 _____ 9/10	8 _____ 9/10

POSITION TITLE: *Department Head/Branch Head* *

POSITION DESCRIPTION: Manages operation of a library unit that is physically separate from the main library (e.g., a branch or a department library) or of one aspect of the main library (e.g., Reference Department, Serials Department, Children's Department).

POSITION TITLE: *(if different from above)* _____

Annual Salary	Annual Salary	Annual Salary	Annual Salary
1 _____ 9/10	5 _____ 9/10	9 _____ 9/10	13 _____ 9/10
2 _____ 9/10	6 _____ 9/10	10 _____ 9/10	14 _____ 9/10
3 _____ 9/10	7 _____ 9/10	11 _____ 9/10	15 _____ 9/10
4 _____ 9/10	8 _____ 9/10	12 _____ 9/10	16 _____ 9/10

* Report only full-time staff *with master's degrees from graduate library education programs accredited by ALA.*

Do not repeat salaries reported in Part I.

POSITION TITLE: *Reference/Information Librarian* *

POSITION DESCRIPTION: Locates information for library users or helps users find it in print materials, automated databases, or other sources. Answers questions and gives instruction about the use of the library. Selects materials for the reference collection and general collections.

POSITION TITLE: *(if different from above)* _____

	Annual Salary		Annual Salary		Annual Salary		Annual Salary
1	_____ 9 10	4	_____ 9 10	7	_____ 9 10	10	_____ 9 10
2	_____ 9 10	5	_____ 9 10	8	_____ 9 10	11	_____ 9 10
3	_____ 9 10	6	_____ 9 10	9	_____ 9 10	12	_____ 9 10

POSITION TITLE: *Cataloger and/or Classifier* *

POSITION DESCRIPTION: Organizes all types of material purchased by the library. Describes each item in standard format and assigns access points. Assigns subject headings and classification numbers. May use automated systems. May be involved with only descriptive cataloging or only subject cataloging/classification.

POSITION TITLE: *(if different from above)* _____

	Annual Salary		Annual Salary		Annual Salary		Annual Salary
1	_____ 9 10	3	_____ 9 10	5	_____ 9 10	7	_____ 9 10
2	_____ 9 10	4	_____ 9 10	6	_____ 9 10	8	_____ 9 10

POSITION TITLE: *Children's and/or Young Adult Services Librarian* *

POSITION DESCRIPTION: Plans and conducts library services for children and/or young adults. Advises on reading materials. Selects materials for the collection. May plan and conduct special programs and outreach services.

POSITION TITLE: *(if different from above)* _____

	Annual Salary		Annual Salary		Annual Salary		Annual Salary
1	_____ 9 10	3	_____ 9 10	5	_____ 9 10	7	_____ 9 10
2	_____ 9 10	4	_____ 9 10	6	_____ 9 10	8	_____ 9 10

* Report only full-time staff *with master's degrees from graduate library education programs accredited by ALA.* Do not repeat salaries reported in Part I.

Part III. SUPPLEMENTARY QUESTIONS

Please help us monitor the library work force by answering the following questions:

1a. Did your library lay off paid staff because of budget cuts in the last 12 months?

_____ yes   _____ no

    1b. If yes, please provide number of full-time equivalent (FTE) staff laid off in the following categories:

    _____ staff with master's degrees from programs accredited by ALA

    _____ all other staff

2a. Did your library lose or freeze vacant positions in the last 12 months?

_____ yes   _____ no

    2b. If yes, please provide the number of full-time equivalent (FTE) positions in the following categories:

    _____ positions usually filled with staff holding master's degrees from programs accredited by ALA

    _____ positions usually filled with other staff

A. Name and title of respondent **: _____

B. Telephone number: (   ) _____

** *Neither libraries nor individuals will be identified in the report of this survey. The name of your library is given here so that we can avoid sending reminders to libraries who respond. The name and phone number of the person responding are requested because we may need to contact him or her if we have questions about this return.*

THANK YOU VERY MUCH! Please return by **April 16, 1993** in the enclosed postage paid envelope to:

American Library Association
Office for Research and Statistics
50 E. Huron Street
Chicago, Illinois 60611

PLACE LABEL HERE

Salaries Paid for Less Than a Twelve Month Year
in Academic Libraries

Instructions on the questionnaire told the respondent: If the incumbent works less than a 12-month year (including vacation), please report the salary and circle the appropriate number of months (9 or 10) for which the salary is paid.

A program was written to prorate these salaries to their twelve month equivalents for the purpose of reporting results of this survey. Table G was created to show how often this process was necessary. The first column shows the total number of incumbents for which salaries are reported in each of the three types of academic institutions on the position tables in this report. The second column shows how many were reported as being for nine months and the third column shows the percentage of incumbents in the category (position/type of library) which that number represents. The following columns repeat that pattern for positions reported as being for ten months and then for a combination of nine and ten month salaries.

Table G.

Salaries Paid for Less Than a 12-month Year in Academic Libraries by Position and Type							
POSITION AND TYPE OF LIBRARY	ALL INCUMBENTS #	9-MONTH #	%	10-MONTH #	%	9 AND 10 MONTH #	%
Director							
Two-year college	132	12	9	7	5	19	14
Four-year college	113	1	1	6	5	7	6
University	228	1		5	2	6	3
Deputy/Associate/Assistant Director							
Two-year college	38	2	5	12	32	14	37
Four-year college	42			3	7	3	7
University	303	2	1	3	1	5	2
Department Head/Branch Head							
Two-year college	36	8	22	2	6	10	28
Four-year college	94	2	2	18	19	20	21
University	1018	24	2	15	1	39	4
Reference/Information Librarian							
Two-year college	147	47	32	14	10	61	41
Four-year college	116	7	6	11	9	18	16
University	982	39	4	19	2	58	6
Cataloger and/or Classifier							
Two-year college	63	15	24	11	17	26	41
Four-year college	55	4	7	6	11	10	18
University	452	12	3	7	2	19	4